YOU LIKE IT DARKER

A Writer's Journal

OVERLOOK CONNECTION PRESS

2024

You Like It Darker: A Writing Journal
© 2024 by Overlook Connection Press.

Dust Jacket & interior Illustrations © 2024 by Glenn Chadbourne.

This is a hardcover, blank journal, featuring lined pages for you to write
your personal or work information. Hard cover journal helps with your
writing no matter where you are, to help keep a steady hand.

Published © 2024 by
Overlook Connection Press
PO Box 1934, Hiram, Georgia 30141
OverlookConnection.com
StephenKingCatalog.com
overlookcn@aol.com

ISBN: 9781623302535

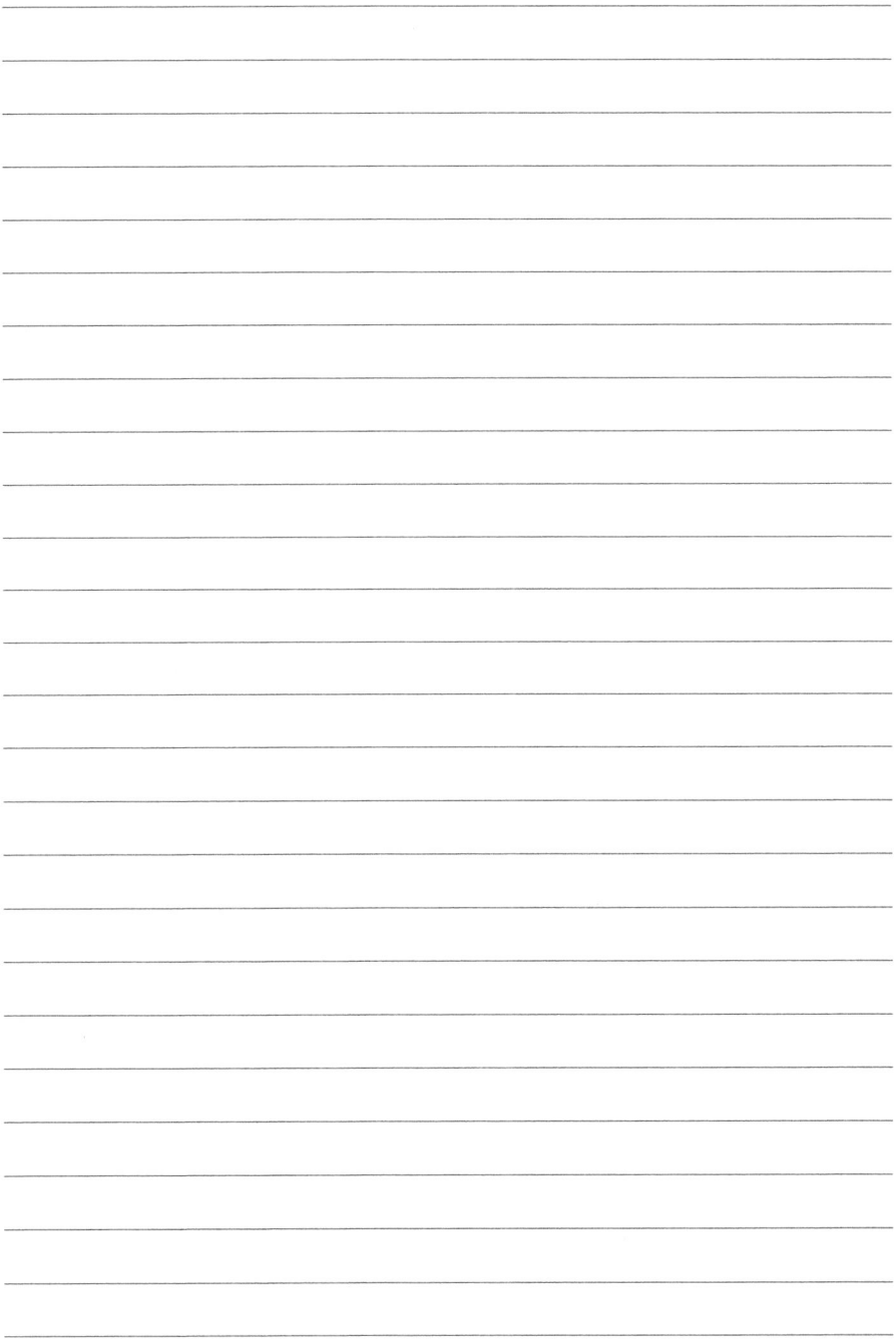

www.ingramcontent.com/pod-product-compliance
Lightning Source LLC
Chambersburg PA
CBHW030510100426
42813CB00002B/424